For   David Thomas—fellow time traveler, teacher and friend
      Karen—weaver and wife

WATER
FROM THE
MOON

.

POEMS
1982- 1989

BY

THOMAS RAIN CROWE

■

New Native Press

Some of these poems first appeared in *Wayah Review, Art Matters, Sun Magazine, Anthology of Magazine Verse 1985, Southern Exposure, Compages, Katuah Journal, Heartland, Birth and Family, Southern ARC, Yearbook of American Poetry 1986, The Mother Earth News, RFD, The Arts Journal, Cold Mountain Review, The Black Mountain Review, The Sound of Light* (cassette).

"Sacred Space," "The Perfect Work," and "The Sacred" were published in *Blue Ridge Parkway: Agent of Transition*, Appalachian Consortium Press, Boone, N.C.
"Chores" was published in *Breadbasket With The Blues*: The American Farmer Series #2; by Seven Buffaloes Press, Big Timber, Montana
"Learning To Dance" and "What Is Woven" were published as broadsides by Landlocked Press, Madison, Wisconsin.
"Seed" was first published as a fine-editions broadside by New Native Press, Sylva, N.C.
"Levitation" was published first as a broadside by Phoenix Graphics, 1982, Houston, Texas

Special thanks to Natalie Scull for her insistence on perfection, proof-reading of manuscripts, and a love of food. And to Ron Arps for his patient typing (and re-typing) of this work.

Acknowledgement to Beacon Press/Boston for use of poem #7 in *The Kabir Book* by Robert Bly (Beacon, 1977) for use as an epigram for the poem "Work" in this collection.

18112

(6.8.96)
c

FIRST PRINTING

New Native books are published for New Native Press. Book orders or information should be addressed to Rt. 67 Box 128, Cullowhee, N.C. 28723.

Book design by Dana Irwin

Front cover painting by Lyn Ott "Balancing of Universal Mind and Universal Heart"

Library of Congress Catalog Card # 93-092605

ISBN 1-883197-03-1

CONTENTS

Preface

PREFACE

"I am nothing; I see all; the currents of
the Universal Being circulate through
me. I am part and parcel of God!"
                                        -Emerson

Years have gone by and I have returned to the world of the
everyday, from the woods. In retrospect, it seems that as a result of my
process and experience of getting "good and grounded" from almost four
years of living a supra-rural lifestyle (very) far from the "madding
crowd" (New Native), I had, in fact, prepared myself for flight into the
realm of the Great Unknown and the currently publicized residential
origins of God! And thusly, my quest for the ultimate answers to the
why's and wherefore's of the causes for Creation—or, as artist Lyn Ott
puts it: "the quest for the face of God"—began. A quest that led me not
only into the minds and theories of some of the greatest rational-logical
minds of our time (which included correspondences with physicist
Stephen Hawking and theologian Thomas Berry), but into the more
ancient intuitive traditions of the East—into the spiraling circle-dance
of the Sufi Dervishes and the inspired and ecstatic language-as-music of
such poet-prophets as Rumi, Kabir, and Hafiz. Here, to me, then as
now, the spiritual traditions of the "pure" poetic flourished and made
pale the modern western literary traditions based in the ideologies of
derangement and debauch. And it was in reading the "ecstatic poets" that
I began, in my own work, to abandon the dark cloud of Aquinas, for the
light! A transition in my life and work. Another Initiation. Another
rite-of-passage that literally led me by the hand from a kind of hanging
uncertainty, to hope, and a new vision for what the healing side of
poetry and the creative could mean. Could BE.
     With the "muse of hope" in tow, my quest for answers to the
questions concerning the origins of "God," to the essential nature of
Source, led me, too, to a project that was not only grounding but that
put me back into touch with the importance of ritual. This 'ritual' took
the form of building a tower—a process that ended up as being as much
spiritual and symbolic as it was physical with regards to work. A tower
that, in all fairness, was as much inspired as it was designed by my
earlier reading of the work and life of Carl Jung, who has had a
profound effect upon any insights I may have had into the world of
perception, and beyond. A Tower. A tower that was the materialization
of a dream. And as it "came true," as it went up, board by board, I was
struck with the wonder of how things make that transition (not unlike
the process of the making of a poem) from the world of 'thought,' from
the world of the unseen, into the world of form and matter—as right
before my eyes this imagined dream-place and refuge for the part of my
soul that writes, was taking-on a 'body' that would soon house the very
desk and typing machine from which I make these words....

I still ask myself, even now, several years after I began writing them, what these poems are about, wondering from where they really came— Whatever the answer to those questions, they seem to be about my own personal and experiential unified-field-theory-of-reality. A theory based upon the belief that poetry (with respect to its process of transmission) is, in fact, a science—a form of notation of Universal Truths and facts broadcast over the illusionary distance of time and space to the opening ears of those of us ready, willing, and able to listen, hear, and transcribe those 'equations' onto paper whether they be in the language-form of mathematics, music, or poetry...for our own use as well as for those struggling travelers yet treading and tripping up the proverbial "mountain path."

As to how I got here to this tower-desk writing this Preface to what will be the last of and the end to almost fifteen years of writing narrative-style poems, as evidenced/chronicled by what I have written over that same stretch of time, I can say, reflectively, that much as *The Personified Street* had been an accounting of my initiation into the world of manhood and western sensibility, and later *New Native* a chronicle of my journey into the world of spirit and Nature (connectedness to place), so *Water From The Moon* is the final leg in a charted journey that maps the travelogue of my personal mythic journey. That leads right up to the doorstep of the present day. An initiatory history of who I am now, and of how I see myself as an equal part and participant of a much bigger Picture, or as Thomas Berry would say, a much more dynamic and symbolic "Story."

Freedom. Truth. Beauty. Destiny. These are all concepts that have preoccupied me for the better part of my life—have taken-on much different and larger proportions, as, simultaneously, everything in my universe has become much smaller, much more personal in a symbolic sense and therefore manageable (or at least, understandable). Yet, paradoxically, and in terms of self-inflicted symbology, my world-view, as well as my writing, has become much simpler, and, in fact, there are fewer and fewer words (images) that seem to speak to, even answer, more and more of those "questions" that keep me up so late and so ever always 'the seeker.' Word-images such as "dance," such as "light." These two words, alone, explain a lot! And there are other images here, in this book, that keep cropping up again and again, almost as if my skills and muscles as a writer had become senile rather than flexed...earth-images referring to the ideas of balance, unity, wholeness—as the "message" seems to be ever more redundant, reverting back to a common beginning from which we, along with all things, come and will return to (in some form) dancing, as light! And rather than to apologize for any lack of imagination with regard to the obvious repetition of certain key words and images in these poems, I have decided to leave them here, as they came, and to arrange them in such a way as to orchestrate this collection, using these repetitions as 'codas,' as 'chorus,' interspersed throughout the natural symphonic cadences and rhythms of the manuscript as a whole. To accentuate not only the ideas that these word-images bring spontaneously to mind, but to allow them to repeat themselves for effect—the same effect that the right kind of repetition in a good piece of music might have in driving-home the point, the _feeling_, of the song.

The poems in this book are all centered with regard to form. I have done this intentionally from the first poem written in 1982, to the last one written earlier this year. I have done this for a very consciously-specific reason. That reason is not to be contrived or to copy anyone else's style, but rather to reinforce what I felt was a necessity for these poems: that they be presented as 'centered' because of the nature of their content. As these poems are about wholeness, unity, and universal order, I felt it was most effective that they should be given that sort of form. Also, most of the poems were written in this form for reasons having to do with punctuation, whereas breath and rhythm are concerned, as the centered form lent itself most organically and musically to the natural rhythm(s) of the individual poem(s).

This book is most essentially, as a whole, I suppose, represented in the poem "What Is Woven," which is a love-song to the interwoven nature of the elements of earth and sky, male and female, spirit and body. A 'tapestry' that uses all the warp and weft that was available to me as 'radio waves,' to poetically weave the rug-of-love upon which all our collective hopes and visions, seductively, lie—an initiatory doormat for a kind of spiritualism that is devoted to unity, yet honors diversity as essential to keeping the loom and the weaver working (growing) through the wee hours of morning, through Time and Space, to their destined and mathematical (and therefore notational) conclusion... To the Beginning which is also, the End. In a world where visions are quietly as commonplace as the taste of water that comes from the moon.

T.R.C.
'Springhouse' 9/89

WATER

FROM THE MOON

"In the eternal darkness, the crow, unable to find food, longed for light, and the earth was illuminated."

-from Eskimo myth

CREATION

for Thomas Berry

In the beginning:
something moved.
And the sound of that moving
filled -up the heavens with dance!

Here is the history of stars:

The power of this music
lit candles along the Backbone of Night.
And the stars were born!
Silent suns welled up in the atoms
of Einstein's sleep.
Gas turned to rock.
Dark rock to the color green.
And we arrived!

Full circle, we come to a new age.
Again, in the spring of this silent stillness,
something will move.
And we'll begin again.
All of us phantoms of flowers.
Pounding out preludes on the clavichord sky.
Lighting the aquarian heavens with dance!

BRILLIANCE

Like the frozen music of lines,
or metal space,
we are trapped in our own ink.
Listening, and not being, the Band.
Watching the snow white brilliance of day
from our windows of silent night.

O BARDS OF BRILLIANCE, COME OUT OF THE CAVE!

We are mad dancing auroras of song.
The listeners of Light.
The eyes of the Great Unknown. Knowing
how our voices are the mirrors for
the ears of the mountains.
And how the mountain sings!

Searching through the soul of streets
we are the Beauty Police.
The bird who finds grain
beneath the blanket of new snow.
The first spring sight of green
in the trees.

Wherever there are beauteous strangers alone,
we are sending blue love through their dreams.
In the form of a lover.
Brilliance.
Or a great song!

THE DECISION

Everything is spinning.
Like mad dervishes in a hoop of light.
As the Earth turns each day
we each go our own ways.
In which direction should we go?

You decide!

One of us is moving toward the silence of trees.
Another, toward water
and the River of Grace.

Slowly, love leads us to the right door.
Inside that house
there are no walls, ceilings, or floors.
Only windows.
And like stones standing at the edge of our own darkness,
we watch
as the night brightly enters our private rooms—

THE DYING

The dying is in the dust.
How the old house covers the shelves
with its age. And the body
starts dreaming of sleep.

Under all this sleepless skin
there is another who is waiting to dance.
A heart
that sings love songs to snow.
And part of a man
wrestling with the wit of God—

Oh Love,
how could we have come all this way
only to die?

I have walked through life with
the feet of a million men.
And only now, in my own shoes,
can I feel the heat of the earth.
As I go deeper and deeper
into the Aztec sun of the fire-soul.
Into the blazen sand of the brain...

Who is listening?

To the groaning of good land.
To the thunder without rain.
To the pride of pleasure,
to the pain—

Meanwhile, night is waiting in the mirrors of memory
for the last dance.
Like being born is the blasphemy of light.
And someday our kisses will begin turning again
to sleep.
The fruit suddenly in love with the wine.
A table, growing old, that has found reverence for the trees.
And the gold that was once our bodies
now dancing in the ancient ashes of
dust into dust....

HOW TO APPROACH THE MOUNTAIN

Go to a mountain
and walk the steepest route to the top.
Then leap from the rock ledge
into the thankless air—
What are you thinking of
as you experience your fall from grace?
A water-soft cloud that will save you
from your poor choice of friends?
A bankroll of blessings from your
favorite saint?

Continue to fall on   and into
the earth.
Now how do you feel about making love
to the corpse of Light?

Everywhere you go to find your way
back to the land of water and sunlight
will only lead to another tunnel's end.
Until you stop dreaming
of falling and of the seduction of rock
and can see yourself approaching the mountain
ready with feet
ready to climb

again for the first time.

WORK

"Knowing nothing shuts the iron gates; the new
love opens them.
The sound of the gates opening wakes the
beautiful woman asleep.
Kabir says: Fantastic! Don't let a chance like this
go by!"

-Kabir

With help, a man can do five times
the work that he can do alone.
With the help of a Friend. Someone
who stands to lose nothing
at ease in the arms of their mate.

Equal in pain, we share in each other's joy.
The way that wings work
together, and the bird flies...

Listen to the sound of the drum with the flute.
As they join hands and
become one thing!
Who has heard a more beautiful sound?

If it seems that your life is going
along an endless and lonesome road, and
the whole earth is balanced, a little crooked
along your back, remember this:

We are not meant to live alone.
For each of us born, somewhere there is
another who knows the truth.
Don't keep staring blindly at the sun! Get to work!
She is waiting for you outside the opening gate!

WHEN THE SNAKE AWAKES BEFORE DAWN

for Joe Napora

Somewhere there is a serpent sliding through
our dreams.
And a mountain
growing from our ancient bodies of rock and clay.
Wherever the snake slides
it takes the mountain.
And wherever the mountain sleeps
is home for the snake—

What is the sound that sits
in the heart of the poet, asleep?
The tune of the goddess
that is making love to a harp?
It is the music of infinity up on its toes.
In love with the beast of rest.

When the snake awakes before dawn
he moves toward the mountain.
Toward the love
shining from a cave of light.
Inside the cave there is a woman
waiting.
Truth, wrapped in music.
About to give birth to the destiny of earth.

The sound of this beautiful music
pulls at the poet's heart, still sleeping.

AND HE AWAKES!

Gifted. Father.
Prophet and Master of the Dream!

WHAT MAN LIVING IN THE EYE OF STONE

What man living in the eye of stone can see
heaven as it bends its wings around earth?
In each other's arms we are as blind as perfect bliss.
As full of peace as a piece of snow.

Now nowhere, not even "hallelujah" reigns
in the brown wren of sunlight covering the cold.
Where no man with a woman need dance to anything
other than, together, their own light!

What is hard in us now is no longer sad.
No longer the dark teeth of what remains.
Unbroken. Fearful. Strange.

How can the gun of sex be anything other than
a man?
A man be anything other than rain?

For forever the stars have promised him Truth.
Knowledge hidden in a language implicit
with lies.
Like churchbells ringing in graves.
Or a man-made moon—

Somewhere in the eye of this rock which is often home,
there is a place that is built for sleep.
A kind of haven from the lack of Light.
A sort of silence from the sound of pain.
Near beginnings.
Not far from "that which ends."
This man in me, that is also "He"
hiding from the moonlight he loves longing

for the Sun!

THE SOUND OF LIGHT

Music is the blood of the stars.
The laugh of God.
The sound of the breath of the moon
in the child asleep.
The sadness of the earth as it sings.
And the yawn of the
old man as he gently dies...

Even the ant is listening to the voice of the sky!
Weaving its way through the grass
in that light.
As Eternity joins in the chorus
of day as it makes love to the night.

All mankind is singing!

Like gyroscopes in the blood of space.
Or luminescence on thresholds of pain.
In the wind, in the trees, in the rain...

Let the colors become the song.
Then sing!

Everyone is singing!
The shepherd. The clown.
The weaver and priest.
And the ones we can't quite see.

All singing.
All in the same key.

Everyone is singing!
The shepherd. The clown.
The weaver and priest.
And the ones we can't quite see.

All singing.
All in the same key.

THE SPEED OF LIGHT

What are words
but the echoes of space.
The prayers of the sun.
Or the rhythms of angels
as they dance to the music of light.

The heart is the bedroom of the soul.
Like the soundless forms on the wall of a cave
to which we pray.
Or the bird that bows down to the Buddha
only looking for grain.

On the suffering side of sleep
eternity is making its bed.
Listen!
To the Silence as it surrenders its wings.
And the dervishes of destiny
as they dance in the new air—

I can no longer censor my prayers!
This ring of silence that surrounds me in sleep.

How quietly the thunder runs through my veins!
Yet how the lightning speaks!

I HAVE SPOKEN MY LAST WORD!

Deep in my chest, breath is giving birth to a rose.
Each petal of that rose, a song.
And every song
only an answer from the eyes.

Where is the earth
when the bear and the river collide?
When the moon and the dust
make peace.

It is in the water in
the old man's eyes.
Eyes that see the Silence
in words.
And the everyday that is moving
past those windows of blood.
Faster than the speed of light!

THE SPEED OF LIFE

Slow down!
Where are you going in such a rush?
To the supermarket of your last dime?
Is the sound of pencilead on paper
too much for your ears?

At fifty miles per hour
the butterfly on the rose by the side of the road
is as invisible
as a wish for the answer to prayers.
As you run through your best years
watching the road.

Faster than the speed of life.

BECOMING BUDDHA

We are all thunderstorms and lightning
waiting to occur.
Children
standing on the steps of the Unknown
gazing toward spring.
Seeds from the garden
becoming food.

As we grow through the rings in our bodies,
the memories dance. Like trees.
Like darkness
dissolving into light.
Knowing, somewhere there inside
that death is giving life a chance.
That freedom is singing its own song.
And birds are not the only ones that fly—

GOD IS A VERB!

And we are moving through timeless space.
Dropping weight of arms
and extra legs along the way. Moving from caves
out into sunlight   like flame.
Like the confidence of wind. Like drying rain...

And we arrive on the circling shoreline of ancient sea
and sing!
Until each of us is
all of us. And all of us
are each of us:

Thunder.
Lightning.

The whole thing!

MOURNING

The greatest yearning is but the reflection
of the greatest hope.

We are all passengers
on our private escalators
climbing the night.

Who will the Hero be?
Man? Woman?
Or the immortal child
born silent in the embrace of our eternal flight.

As I speak the secret word:
the sky is becoming a part of my hands!
Don't cry! We are not alone.
The ones we weep for
will return as children. And light!

FOOD

When the wind blows over the face of the sea
it turns to rain.
And the rain blowing becomes waves.
The waves rushing back and forth
through the streets of the water-world
is like the mind asleep.
Only when the sea is calmed and
the wind becomes nothing more than a breeze
do the birds fly out from the land
and feed—

Yet, even the River Niger cries out in the voice of pain!
As its people bow down to the god of Food.
As the old ones lie hot in the sand
next to the shells of the young.
As the grain trains roll by
towards tables of wealth.

O Africa, why is the sky
turning now as dark as
the color of your skin?

When the wave wants to become the water,
the wind blows.
And everywhere everything begins to dance:
The wind with the salt
becomes foam.
And the foam with the earth
that becomes the shore—

EVERYTHING IS MOVING!

The sand, the water, the rock,
the bear, the human child, the whale, the wind and the oak.
And the coming and going of the waves...
Like a baker who is mixing grain with milk.
Dreaming of bread.

ENOUGH TO FEED ALL THE HUNGRY ON EARTH!

AMNESIA

My mind and body have gone to sleep.
And the past is neither a part of my dreams
nor that which I see when I awake.
And all I remember is
what I have felt strongly.
Only the fingers and lips
of the love song.
Only the salt of tears and
the ache in the throat from
laughing all night.

Where has it gone?
The time between getting up for work
and paying the rent. And the list of names
of all those things without names which are
like the words we have given to rocks
to describe the way we die.

Now, it is the genius of forgetting
that has made me dumb
so that my heartbody may come alive!
And as this door opens in
the room of drawn shades,
I am there with
the memory of the lover I will soon for the first time meet.
On the first bus that
comes to the bustop. The last woman
who will leave from the party to go home
alone.
Or in a picture on the wall of a deserted store
that through the cracked and cloudy glass
is calling out my name.

WHAT IS WOVEN

for Karen

It's like the way the wool is thread
into the arms of the loom that I love you.
How each strand of silk is a step
in the dance of the way you weave
has me married to this dream of cloth—

What is brought together in embrace
is woven.
The bond of warmth in winter's bed.
Or the white
lightly flowing in the hair of a bride.

The parts of the whole in a piece of cloth
are the strings that come to me as kisses.
A million lips that have sculpted my face.
And in black and white I am the gift of the rug
that lays in reverence at your feet.

With the rhythm of the silent song the loom sings,
I am learning to talk to the moon.
To the sun and stars.
And to the trees the secret words of the dance...
Oh love, what pattern are we weaving with
the back and forth of this dance?
Not until this spinning wheel of yarn
has run out will we know the form
that together we will take:
The *weft* of one body that's free!

That which is completed together
is woven.
Woven as the wood in a window to glass.
And the way that my heart is sewn to your door
I will love you:
a piece of morning
sleyn and embroidered on the *reed* of night!

WHEN THE SIDEREAL ESSENCES

When the sidereal essences
and the river stones talk
to the moon it is time for the dance!
The sounds of women near fire.
Or men
that are huddled in caves
listening to the heartbeat of Earth.

Whenever she calls my name
I return to my past. To the graves.
The eye of a rattle
or the spirit of forgotten stone—

Like the omen of change in the owl
I have heard her:
moving like the life work of water beneath dirt.
Like the color red in the rain.
Or the sun turned silver
from the black voice of the moon!

Touched by the sun, I have lived in silence.
Because silence is full of screams.
When I drink of the water
I hear the river stones talking to the moon.

IT IS TIME FOR THE DANCE!

As dawn grows through the middle of night
like ancient beans....

FALL FROM GRACE

Fall is the season of the poem!
The cold breeze of the mind
as it talks to the earth
in the language of fallen leaves—

Were I to have but one name for the changing trees
it would be "God."
Were I to have but one bowl for my morning rice
it would be made of wood.
Were I to have but one path
through the woods to the place where I go to pray
it would be along the stream.
Were I to have but one robe to keep this body warm
it would be made of the finest wool!

No matter where we go to be alone,
beauty is living there too.
The way excellence stands guard
at the door of a poor man as if he were rich.

When I say to the woman I love, "I love you,"
all she hears is the voice of my pain.
It is when I reach for her hand that my heart speaks!

What is summer saying to this fall?
Is it some sweet goodbye?
Is it the list of names
winter is wearing in the hidden seams of its coat?
Or the lullabye of an ancient kiss?

It is this:
From the seed that once gave birth to the tree,
to the tree we will return and embrace.
Each year. As fallen leaves.
From grace!

GOING HOME

Suppose everything we know
is false.
Our bodies are not our bodies. Rivers not
rivers. And air not really air—
But something else.

Imagine the world as a shadow
of another life.
Where there are no sweet smells of food cooking.
And no food. Where there are lovers
kissing. And no lips. And no lovers.
Where there is no such thing as darkness
or light. Only eyes....

The dream we imagine to be our lives,
is just that: a dream.
Each of us is a drop of water. A part
of an endless sea.
When we are swimming in that ocean, we become that sea.
Only when we walk out of that sea
are we alone,
and are bound to the limits of this life.

The sound of waves reaches the ears of the unborn Child, asleep.
Yet, there is no sound. The ringing the shepherd hears
in the high meadow, from the bells
around the necks of each of his sheep, is a wonderful music!
Yet, there are no bells—

We are all working our way back to The Sea.
Where everything lives. Nothing exists.
And we're free!

ILLNESS

The mind and the body are one.
A city, full of all kinds of life.

In alleys and in dim-lit bars
the thugs of illness dance.
Sharpening their knives
and waiting for their chance
to rob us.
To inflict our poor bodies with pain—

When we want to be sick
our body will usually agree.
Easy to please,
criminals will appear at every door.
The dogs of disease in every ditch.

What does this mean?

As we open our lives to new things
we run the risk of darkness slipping in.
Learn to know and love this pain.
Like rain is to earth
and helps the rose to grow.
So stand strong in the streets of your own illness.
Until those fragile urban roads that are widening
turn to Autobahns of light!

FOR THE FEATHERS IN THE HEALER'S FAN

*"Any idea, person or object, can be a Medicine
Wheel, a Mirror for Man. The tiniest flower
can be such a Mirror, as can a wolf, a story, a
touch, a religion, or a mountain top."*
                                    -Hyemeyohsts Storm

This is the one that flies.
The one with wings
with every man's heart in its hand.

And this one is wind.
The one that breathes,
the holy breath, that moves through all things—

This is the one that cares. The soothing blue
in the twilight of every eye.

And this: the flame. The fire gone
wild in the streets of wild dance.
The seam in the blouse of night—

This is the one that dreams.
Kisses stolen from the rain. Or the voice
within books.

This is the one that cries.
A cup of tears. On tables for those who pray
.   and weep for the water in food.

And this one sings!
New songs to the planet Earth. Of new death,
new life, and new birth—

This is the one that heals. Heaven's hands
reaching down from the drumbeats of space.
Light from the wheel.
Dressed-up in the fashions of grace...

And here, the one that laughs. The river in the rock.
The giver of good things to those
lost in the darkness of their own joy.

And which one is this, hiding
behind all the other feathers in the fan?
It is the one that dies. The one that tunes his bow
to the strings of death. Who takes lightly the lives
of all trembling and arrogant men.
And like the one that flies, comes back,
to live again!

The rest are the ones that dance.
In the shadows of the healer's full moon fire.
At the edge of the lake. Its blood beating
time on the tambourine shore. To each dancer and dance
sculpting the sand with their dreams.

REMEMBERING OUR KIN

for Gelolo McHugh
(1907-1981)

Heaven is in the heart.
Edens, and pastures of endless green.
And nothing but soothing light.

Through the gateway to the West,
death is driving darkness to the grave.
To corncribs of night.
Toward the final thunder of all our collective
dreams.

In the corners of the planet Earth,
nexus is holding its dance.
Listen, as the spirits of all animals and
the hearts of all men
bounce in perfect rhythm in the dirt!
As the resurrection bird sings
swansongs to an ancient caste.
And the wind is blessing the air with its wings—

The ashes we are spreading through this grass
is food for the rain.
A special mulch for the mist.
And the crickets and the robins
sing!

So long, old friend.
The space you are leaving, empty, behind, is slowly filling
like a springbed of love in this rain.
Here.
Where we are all Family in this place.
Drunk on and drinking from the stream.

INSIDE LONELY SONG

for Eugene Friesen

Here, the loud silences of skin
is the prison of cells.
How the exiled voice of the moon
is singing dirges to the death of words.
Like lost atoms
looking for the home of destiny in the enormous body of God.

Somehow the electric strings of space
keep on playing their tune.
And the man of waves
or the woman of light
together become song!

What is the music of Love
but the sound of a single note that has found itself in the song?
Even the old ant
finds his way through the grass,
following the path of this gifted voice,
and is Home!

Flower, petal, eagle and wing
are the parts and the players
of sorrow.
This loneliness inside music.
Perfect, yet only part of the part we see.

What are lips if not for kissing?
Tongues, if not for the taste of something sweet?
Teeth, if not for learning the
whistles of grace?

Together they are the cello of song!

A lonely box of wood.
Enflamed, by the hands of he who plays it.
With fingers of fire dancing
to the chorus of unknown tears.
Falling from the moon....

TO KILL SHADOW

I want to kill my shadow!
All morning it follows me through town
like a beggar demanding my dimes.
And all afternoon
it follows me around
just out of sight.

What will women think of a man who
hangs out with such a pest?

I have a plan.
Let's all change our names to "night."
Wear dark suits. And stay inside
all day.

Everywhere, shadows will be starving.
Crying-out in stomach pain.
Praying for forgiveness.
Asking questions.
Lost in their own light.

BREAKING NEW GROUND

A year older now,
I watch as the new spring air changes my life.
Pronounces me dead. Or takes without asking: my wife.
For the earth needs water too!
And no tear's blood ever mingled shyly with the rain—

Scoop by scoop, shovel by shovel, an old life
is buried as new ground is exposed to new light.
Like memories turning over in their grave. Like shadows on the pages
in a late night book.

When I'm gone, and trees again cover this land
I now work with sweat and love,
I'll still be watching.
Watching from out there, beyond. Or
from the old oak at the edge of these woods.
As another young man
with axe and spade in his hands looks out over
what will soon be a garden field.
Grass growing up there right before his eyes.
Inside.

FIRST LIGHT

Here in mountains
or in pastureland of stars
the fires of genesis dance
in the galaxies of a single stone.
In an atom that was once
a sun.
And was burning in the first perfect moment
of heat.

How can something simple as love
be measured by eons of expanding light?
A wisp of wind become breath for the sea?

Only in the darkness of ancient evening did she dance
in firelight to the music of his eyes.
Like a billion years without skin
that suddenly in an instant became body burst into flames!

How it must have been the first time
the sea made love to the thought of rain!
The first time God   entered space—
And the woman in water gave birth
to the seed of corn,   of sacred leaf...

Even in the evening she dreams of morning
in her sleep. Of that quiet moment before love
when creation paused
at the thought of dawn flooding his face.
When hands become legs and
bodies become the moving waves of sheets
covering the darkness before the birth of stars!
Before even the breath of Truth
became flames dancing from the dream
on fire in a poet's heart

And there was light!

LIKE BIRDS NOT EVEN LIFTING THEIR WINGS

Like wires running through the air of dirt
we have spoken to our oldest, to our most
ancient thoughts.
Words
that fly like birds not even lifting their wings
we pass our dreams on to kindred light.

Some highway-to-heaven this road we live in
or on as 'the body of Man!'
Some kind of burning flesh
that joins gravity, in jest, to the laugh of night.

From the mountain, deep inside there are
signals sending lovesongs to the brain of the earth.
Shooting pains from the heartcore of crystal
to the eyes of water   called "tears."

Listen, to the lullabyes of the deserted Mother's voice of pain!
How the sad songs rhyme with the blue-green dirt.
How the soaring heartbeat of hope echoes the refrain of heat!

On a hill of stone near the sea
an old man sits with the tickle of his last hair.
With the kiss of a sea's sweet wind which is also rain.
He is listening to the voices coming
over the airwaves of earth. From the other side of the sea.
Of old grayhaired men and women in love with the moon

that with the voice of sunlight are calling out his name!

SACRED SPACE

for Michael McClure

The lake in the room of death
is on fire.

The tiger is eating my legs.
And the desert is quiet
now with the memory of
my blood.

On the avenues at night
women are calling my name.
"Love," they shout
from the corners of the House of Lights—

What if God were governor
of these states?
How would the stars in our dreams
or the eyes of Isis dance
in the memories of police?

TOO MANY CARS IN MY BLOOD!

Somewhere is a piece of land where
all of silence plays drum.
Where greed is a shade of blue
each night that covers my sleep.
And lust is the gift of milk
from a goat.
These traces are like the silhouette of lightning
in hands.
The eyes of a brick.
Or the sacred spot where eventually
everything stands.

NEAR A PLACE OF POWER

Wherever there are worlds where I belong
I am ready to go.
To lie down on the mountain
and travel its paths through the laurel of sleep—

Lying there,
where underground the veins of water meet
and birds and turtle come to die,
I had a dream...

...I saw the spirit of Beauty sex-bought at Banks.
I touched pain in the beds of painless sleep.
I smelled the sweet perfumes of waste not wasted.
I tasted jealous rage from the spoons of joy.
Heard roses crying death
from their cars—

HOW DOES A TREE KNEEL
WHEN IT IS READY TO PRAY?

Like the echoes of the first man
off mountains we can no longer see,
the wind carries our thoughts,
like secrets, to the ears of God.
And hidden inside
we are as easily seen
as it is easy to open a book,
as public
as the portrait of a great king.

Knowing this, I awake on the breast of the mountain.
Gathering milk from a spring.
Collecting my past
from the bones of animals
that have come to say their last prayers
at the feet of rock.
On this mountain.
In this water.
At the altar of a dream.

SUNSINGER

for Paul Winter

What I say
are only the things I meant to say
and have written in words.
A lovely music. Something still imprisoned in stone.
A piece of wind hung up like a
kite in the trees.
Or the fish who
fights its own image in glass.
And the god
hiding beneath the flesh of a man
who can do anything, yet is lost
in finding nothing he wants to do.

Where is this "heaven" they talk of in books?
All these possums and wolves. Roses
growing from the lawn   like grass—
It must be hidden in the brilliance that
comes from the Sun! In the golden gleam of light
we don't see yet feel
as the melody of heat.

Heaven is where songs come from.
Where music is made to the god and goddess
of Light.
And what makes me a singer of the song
that history has only written in words.
That rises like daylight and eagles over the mountains
sunsinging solos   to the tune of this blinding night!

TRIAL BY FIRE

"Love sets on fire the one who finds it."
-Meher Baba

On the wings of a wish
we drove into the mouth of Christmas.
Toward the calm
near the eye of a storm.

Only a moment through the doors of Eden
and a greeting of flames!
Balls of fire from the furnace
and my body clothed in the teeth of orange light.
As fantasy turned to nightmare
in a flash!

As the beauty of this solstice gift of peace
began its destructive journey of heat,
and anger began to replace the woman in your eyes;
somewhere in the smoke rising from these hills
an angel stood fanning out the fire with her wings.
And streams of water fell, wonderfully,
from the Master's bath.

From this trial by fire
we have plumbed, painted, and re-kindled our love.
The blessing of this Christmas spent alive and still shared
through the giving of gifts.
Through food.

With the fire out
and the smell of smoke gone from our blood,
WHAT HAVE WE LEARNED?
Yet, we awoke this morning, warmed by your dreams.
A column of light.
Like a standing furnace of Love
that has lit the logs of our lives
without flame.
As a gift on this birth day
from God.
And a test of our love
by fire.

PIECES. OF THE REAL THING

I am liquid next to
your love
because I am not your love.
Love next to your body
because I am not yet whole.
Whole next to
your pieces
because I am not your eyes.
Eyes next to your heartbeat
because I am not your flame.
Child next to your flame
because I am not your fire.
Fire next to
the way you leave me
alive with my sadness
because I am not your sadness.
One next to your quiet love
because I am not Love.

Because I am only

pieces

of every part

of what is only

the only

real

thing.

And it's the way you make me
shy,
silent,
strong
that makes my silhouette white against
all this darkening land.
And so,
I am colours next to
your darkness.
Halos
next to your light.
Kisses
next to your kissing.
Because I am not you kissing.
And at night
how our sleeping body shines!

LEARNING TO DANCE

for N. N.

I am disappearing
into the side of her body.
Her body, which when it lifts
and turns, also moves the Earth.
I have given up the toys
of my childhood
and my ambitions for old age.
And have moved deep within
the walls of her silver skin.

I am through with my love of suffering.
And the words that describe that love.
I am going to carry on a magnificent
affair with the wind
      from the inside of her body
      where we both sleep.

Friends, I am going deeper, even
      deeper inside than the animal
      or a blade of grass—
I am looking for the stones.
The stones that lay to the side
and in the bed of the Great River.
Among those stones
there is only one rock with my name.
I will pick it up
and hold it high above my head
in the inner light.

I will know many things.

Outside, with her body, she
is teaching the world to dance!

LEARNING TO DIE

To be prepared for dying,
and yet live! the wise ones will say.
And so I go on.
Too busy to stop and cry, or
sometimes to even rest.
Ice ages come and go between each breath
as I hoe the corn rows.
Mountains
rise up and then melt again into sand
in the time it takes to drink
one drink from the pure stream that runs nearby.

How can my friends find time
to dream of being rich?
To bad-mouth the moon.
Or chase women around all day—
I tell them that good sex is
having only a small house to sweep.
And a bowl of hot soup at the end of the day.

They think I am foolish
living alone out there in the dark and wolf-ridden woods.
And they go on with their dying.
More lonely than any moonlit night.

Back in my forest home,
I sit by the fire and listen to the rain
falling from the maples onto the roof.
I am learning to die from the simple things
that keep me each night from sleep.
In each shadow that dances through the woods.
Preparing for the day when darkness
makes of me a feast.
Knowing this, I am "infidel," "godless heathen." Zero.
But still live!

THE REAL WIND

Imagine a kind of wind that blows in Space.
What is the color of that wind?
Is it something with a name?

I am talking about the birth and death of a breeze.
A breath of air.
Light
inhaled by the mouth of the sun.

Ideas are like small pieces of soft rock
falling into the mind from beyond.
As soon as they touch the earth,
they're gone...

Where will we be
when the earth changes, again,
to air?
When our bodies are nothing
but that lonely breeze?
I think we'll all be
the poetry of some magic work.
Spades in an endless soil.

Digging destiny from the speed of light!

THE PERFECT WORK

Love is the perfect work.
A music which rings all the bells in the temple.
A special wind in the trees—

Listen to the way the drummer hits
lovingly his drum.
The way the dancer moves
over the warm earth.
And watch as children
leave their bodies behind on the old logs
around the fire and sing!

The world is aglow in the shadows of the
children singing. Of the sticks against
wood. Of the heavy silent breathing of the old ones
who sit off to the sides of the circle and pray.

When I am at work in my garden
I take off my shoes. I let
my other hands embrace dirt.
I plant myself in this place.
And knowing what love is, I
awake. In this place in my body.
Full of dream music,
Full of light!

THE LAST WORD

If I could wake completely,
I would say without speaking
why I'm ashamed of using words.
                    -Rumi

Darkness rolls into the mind like
another army aiming to rule the Earth. And

millions of years separate the first mother's womb
and the sound of children being born now in glass.

Do any of us remember the sound where silence began
amidst the noise of these buildings crying out in pain?

A thousand songs or Christ arriving for the hundredth time
to our world cannot bring peace.

And those of us alone in the woods are trying to live
beyond words.

WHAT SPEAKS

Weeping is the language of the soul.
The first word.
Or the passion of a poet to see, with his own eyes,
the wind.

Words are but the fences 'round the house of Truth.
Does the sun talk?
Does the moon cry?
What speaks?

Like the block of wood
which changed in his hands
from a vulture to a dove,
the old man spoke of peace.
The movement of the knife with the grain
was a thing of beauty. Like a mouth
that gathers water from the source of a mountain spring.
Like warpaint across the nose of the earth.

WHAT IS MAN?

We are the brain cells of God.
The stars in the sky. And
every thought. From the beginning of time:
All the same—

While the woman who is weaving her orphaned strands
into a family of cloth, listens to the loom;
somewhere a man ties feathers to his favorite drum.
And in that distance
the union of that moment speaks.

As he tells her in the language of
skin entering skin of his love,
at that moment in the heavens a galaxy draws its first breath.
And on a sacred piece of earth
a boy or girl is born, like a star.

What speaks?

Is it the music that is turning next into light?
The wind
that will come again as the tree?

What is man?

I think it is you.
It is I.
It is WE!

RETURNING AS RAIN

When you cried
your tears rose up again from the earth
into what we called 'heaven'
and became clouds
clouds of rain
rain which fell back on us and our gardens
which was you!

You stood there between rows of corn
and the rich earth. Replenishing yourself
as the draught of God. Making manna from tears of the moon.

From where has this storm of beauty come
that has given such good sex to these eyes?
Such pleasure
to the bodies of heaven and earth!
What price must now we pay
to see you cry? To watch the wet miracle of birth.

When your last tear has finally touched the last dry grain of dirt,
where will you be in this fantasy's daydream of light?
Wherever you go
I will still be watching.
Waiting for every cloud that moves from behind the mountain
with your eyes. With the promise of you,
returning as the rain.

CIRCULATORY

Wherever there is one man singing,
there is wind.
Something moving around in the air.
As if it were blood.
Moving with passion to the point of sex.
Toward the shadow of pain.

But not even the dead ones
really know pain.
That silent noise
where the living and the almost dead don't meet.

Just as sure as a circle has a date of birth,
and the prophecy of air   becomes dust,
all things begin.
Twist and turn to the sun
like the cool music that comes from caves.
The life of a book.
Or Beauty
emerging from the stains in glass.
Where any man who has really known love
returns.
To where the wheel and the singing have joined
to become song.
Become broken breath.

Shattered sweetly on the lips of the dance.

WATER FROM THE MOON

for Lyn Ott

Like the fire that speaks from a tree,
only he who has met God may walk
through this life with the eyes of a saint.
Why do we wait
'til the wind has died and the storm has passed on
to speak the truth?
Surely something more than a piece of wood
will from the history of war
bring peace!

Just as the ferns near the quiet water
unwind toward the warm sun of spring,
the sky opens its veins to the mountains
and bleeds.
And all that is living
is nourished in the bath of blood!

What we know
is only the mirror in still water
of what we will never see.
Our lives.
A kind of Death.
That threatens the wires that now carry our light
with a darkness
that comes from machines.

Yet, only a single word from the tree
will bring water from the moon.
Speech from a rock.
And the man who knows everything
in the nothing of the mind
will for no reason known
see God!

IN THE DREAM AFTER SLEEP

Nothing
is the dream.
And Everything:
the dreamer. Through the eyes of the world
we see when we arise.
Even though we are all asleep,
there is something larger awake in our dreams.

Beyond the solitary state of all sleep,
God dreams of dessert.
The pie after all the fruit is gone.
The bath of wind
that in these bodies of clay we know as rest.

Is it really the sleep
that brings us unclothed to these beds?
And that same sleep
that morning opens like southern windows
into northern light?

We are all riders on this daydrift
through night. Weavers
of this woven dream, that dies.
While we sleep, lifetimes and circus trains of stars
are going by outside.
Elephants becoming ants.
And ants growing up into trees.

AWAKE!

We are all of these!

BIRTH

for Califia

On the lake at night
the swan swims away from the hungry man.
Swimming circles around the silhouette shadow of moon.
A moon smiling, from its sanctuary of water away from
the shore.

In her body
the wilderness dances with spring.
And it is only the sunlight
that has intoxicated day into night
with each dawn
when she awakes to the taste of new wine.

Look how fast this body grows
in the basket of her mother's womb!
Like ears of corn on the stalk
suddenly ready to be picked.
And like a comet's ride through space
the new one falls into the bowl of life.
Into the moonlit lake of wine,

and is born!

WHERE THERE ARE WHEELS
TURNING IN THE WIND

Where there are wheels turning in the wind
nearby there is water.
Blue water.
And also the earth, and air.
Like arms
that wrap around the boy or girl about to be born
to explain the secrets of life.

How can we even guess
the birthplace of this dream which will give name to new life?
The blessed seed
that in spring will crawl from its mother's earth
in search of its own face, mirrored in sun!

Yet in our ignorance,
there is one who knows the Truth.
It is the one inside
wrapped in innocence waiting to be born.
Who comes into our lives fresh and singing:
the rose-god again in a body.
Petalswept in silence to the key of Earth!

EQUINOX

Only the rain
comes today between my eyelids and the light.
And not even music
knows the chords of the code to my door.

As the rain turns to sunlight
the moon is washing day from the sky.
And the mirror that beauty seeks
has become water to a man with great thirst.
Like a vein of gold, unfound.

In the earth, as in the sky, there are echoes of dreams.
And the falcon in these woods
is waiting for the sound of drums.
The springbranch
for the voice of a flute.

See how quickly our mind becomes water
as we gaze at the moon!

Like the phoenix that is also the dove
we will finally fall into the place where we belong.
Like the seasons.
Like ocean. Like sand.
Or like music that comes from the warm tears of rock.

At home in the star-earthen sky!

GROWING

When the ground within you is warmed
it is then that the sleeping seeds will grow.
And we come out of our winter shacks
into spring.
Into our gardens. Filling
compost in every row.

How green the grass is
as it covers the head of the earth!

Where there are weeds in the heart,
a heavy mulch will keep it free. Keep rain in the roots.
And warm like a quilted bed.

Each plant in your garden is a voice, waiting
to share with you its song. They are lovesongs from
another place. From fertile ground. From space—

Harvest your food as if each plant were
fresh from its mother's womb of crystal, quicksilver, and gold.
Destined for the netherworld of our bodies
of blood in the air.

Now give thanks for the gift that enters you fresh.
And the waters that wash it down.

We are living in the rows of our own gardens.
Every day.
Strengthening and enriching the soil!

ENLIGHTENMENT

Sometimes
the only way to enlightenment
is to sleep on the bed of an over-thrown dictator
who longs for the deep lush banks of the river.
Even the women know
the only time to make love is in the cusp of the night.
The spring is creeping over the hills of destiny
with the food of tomorrow's need in its teeth.
Rama and Krishna are the war lords of yesterday.
Only the new saviour in the heart of modern man
can be crucified on Sunday in the pulpits
of institutional greed.

"Come and follow me!"

said the giraffe
as the monkeys of dawn knocked at their doors.
And the parade of stars traveled through the night
to neverneverland on the backs of a Dream.

SEED

From hands that have learned to scratch the
soil like another skin,
the seed slips into the wounded earth.
Like a prophet who lays down by water
and begins to dream...
the seed begins to take on new life.

WE ARE ALL SEEDS!

A piece of grain
between the forefinger and the thumb of God.
The cold fire of night
that gives life to the soul of dying wood.
And the voice of rain, as light,
as it enters and makes love to the earth.

How wonderful that this small round seed could grow
into the majesty of a great tree!
Into the face of a flower.
Or the sweet taste of something to eat.

WE ARE ALL SEEDS!

Circles
reflecting rainbows 'round the sun.
Where a smile is brother to a sister's kiss.
And prayer is the face
we will one day know as peace.
Growing from the prophet's dream of the garden.
Becoming the forests and fields.

Surrounding the old mountains with life!

THE DEATH OF DESCARTES

*Everything that has already happened is
particles; everything in the future is waves.*

Move through your past as if
the days were dropping leaves.
And this, the last day of Fall.
When all the world hides from
its own wealth. And the new love,
like the wind,
impregnates your dreams!

What a healthy sound that will be!
Like a million octaves that hug in the night
becoming a single tone.
Like the waves in all the world's oceans
crashing together on the same shore.

Today is a good day!
Even the blackbird has a hip song.
Even the old brown bear is out wandering away from his winter home.

Tomorrow, I'll be back again swinging
somewhere between heaven and earth.
Lost, somewhere inside
or in the woods far from my cabin door
thinking of food.
But today, I am here. Near the breath and shadow of sun.
Visiting wind that has come home to old familiar trees.

I *FEEL*, THEREFORE I AM!

Like walking through water
falling from the side of a mountain
and then hugging a warm body of heat.

Tonight I'll just sit in moonlight
by an open fire. And watch the sky.
Translating poems in the language of stars!

TRUTH

I.

"What ain't the truth is a lie,"
the old man would say.
Two things
moving against each other around
the circle of night.

Years went by
and I began to notice how for some things to live
other things died.
How the food in my garden grew
side by side with the weeds. How
the hawk hunted the rabbit, and yet
the rabbits lived!

Inside, something was growing. Something
was being born.
And each day I felt
the gentle tug of that pain.
Like the hands of hunger near bread.
Or the rain...

Now I know! I have seen it in my own face.
And in the eyes of the smallest ant, or
in the grace of a bird on the wing:

that the Truth is the shape of a ring; all
of us equal, and all of us only

one thing!

II.

What ain't the truth is a lie.
As if daylight were the nexus of night.
And all joy
was but the mirror of some perfect pain.

What would truth be
without lies?
An empty room.
A station without the sound of trains.

Just when we think we know the truth,
Eternity takes off her mask.
Lets us look at her eyes.

And I am back inside the silence of
a heart that snores in its sleep.
It has been another long day.
The hay is all raked.
The orchards pruned.
Last night I dreamed I was an eagle
circling the sun!

LETTING LOVE FAIL

Somewhere, a man or a woman is waiting to love you.
Will your blindness ever reveal to you
any open door?

If pain has closed your eyes
to new things, then how are you going to see?

Come out of the cave!

Open the windows of your heart to this new spring.
The wind is out there too. Let it in.
It has a million poems for you
it wants to recite. And thousands of kisses and dreams—

With your hands up over your ears, your lover's voice
will pass you by like lost silences
dancing blindfold in the night.

BLIND LOVE

A long time without love,
I set the stage for this romance.
Roses by the fire. White wine in the crystal glass.
And my best shoes.

How will I know if she loves me
without taking this chance?
Of crawling out, again,
onto that fragile limb.

What if she doesn't dance!
Hates my shoes.
Or finds the wine too cold.

I see it like this: when we bait the trap of love blindly,
who knows what we will catch!

LOVE AT THE SPEED OF LIGHT

I.

Maybe it was only yesterday's
Indian moon that drew me into the
Courtyard of your smile
Always lingering there like the strings of the music on love's guitar.

Just imagine together the kind of tune we might play
Entertaining that moon
And her cousin the sun, with the sound of our kisses
Nearing the horizon. Traveling at the speed of light!

II.

Maybe it was the moon that night
In the mountain sky that
Came into my heart and set that lonely fire with
Another man's name on the wood. And it's all

Just because you're there and there is no
End to the dying embers still rolling around in my chest
Always burning, always brighter, and for weeks
Never going out.

III.

Moments are only small eternities covered
In the silent centuries of your grace.
Cannons going off in the gunneries of
Another autumn day like a memory medicine men have conjured
with love.

January has gone on long enough and
Eternity is weeping at night with
All the pain that distance brings when you're gone, and
Nothing will change the death of this little lie that is you in me,
that lives!

DOLPHINS

for: the imagined One

I.

D own at the edge of twilight twisting and dancing

O ver the mist in perfect waves we

L ong to become what we are in the aren't of

P eople in the form of fins whistling our names and

H ow we reach out to touch the silky wetness of skin

I n this dream of talking without words or even

N oise that has somehow become the sound of ocean

S omewhere where there is no water and I am lost in your eyes.

II.

D o we ever really do the right thing when

O ur eyes meet and

L ips want to be hands if only to feel

P ast the feeling of being touched, toyed with, tickled

H ere where only a heart beats

I n the middle of me learning to swim out beyond the

N owhere of waves making light of the undertow knocking about in my brain

S o loud that deafness almost sounds like a kiss.

III.

D awn moves like an arson into the end of night with

O ur bodies bent like bullets moving through the shattered reflection of glass

L ong legs jealous of arms intertwined in a dance that can only be

P art of what an ocean wears to bed with

H alf a moon for light lighting your face

I n ways that only a man in love with himself can see

N ot as something water would wrestle away from the dead like

S oft pearls stealing innocence from these fingers robbed of your smile.

IV.

Let's D o what the dolphins do and dance

O ut where the waves are nothing but a

L ovesong's tears wearing away the sand the way

P irates take beauty away from its toys and

H old it for ransom the way I would hold you

I n my seasick arms if only we were two ships

N earing the edge of night where only the eyes of dolphin shed light on

S omething as bright as a dream!

OH LOVE

Oh love,
where do you go with your silence?
I am moving into
the infinite walls of your skin
in search of our being.
Only this oneness knows
eternity's secret to prayer.
Or the music of spheres
which I have seen whirling in your eyes.

From a sacred rock
together we saw the ancient dance of stone.
How the mist reveals the mountains
and the mountains move!

Somewhere through the non-existent doors of my heart,
an eagle will fly,
and this race of wind in my mind
will cease.
And there again we will meet.
God looking God in the eye.
On the first full moon of fall.

You have come to me
like the very first beat of my heart.
The first breath.
Or happiness
showing itself in tears
or smiles that will forever glow!

Oh love,
as I move deep into the gardens of your dreams,
you are still asleep in me.
Every miracle that a man with a woman can be.
You are everything!
Sight. Sound. Touch.
And the Ancient One
walking in silence from the sea—
You are everything:
The silence.
The song.
And the one inside that is me!

WEDDING SONG

Where the river is forgotten is
where he lays flowers on
the grave of the thought of her gone. A river.
A river for her and the tears
before even blood could blink and
they become one and the same
sex. The grass mingled with the moss.
The moss meandering down hillside
into the hollars called home. Home
where heart means all the miles of
lessons learned now forged into
the shape of a ring. A ring ringing
like song. A song singing like sin was
before hell opened its gates to love.
And love arrived.

Vows. Vowels only of the verb to be.
To be and be born babes
in the air of eternal youth.
Wind. Windows as wings flying into
the breath of the end of a kiss.
Caring. Carrying water uphill
to the roots hidden in this mountain meadow
of grass.

Why do they whisper to the rain?
In their love they take each other in.
The silent river running through their legs
to the sea—

Where he bends.

She waits.

They are water for the seeds.

THE NEW DANCE

Dancing, I have finally found my feet.
My head and hands.
And the woman who is no longer there
as I find in the whirling, a new love.

Somewhere, there is a Race which only sings.
On a planet where it does nothing but snow.
Somewhere, there is a people that only smiles.
In a world where all they know is rain.
Somewhere, there is a country that can only be seen
through the silent veils of a kiss.
In a land that is nothing but light.
Somewhere, there is a man whose only language is the dance.
In a life where all things are in a state of dancing.

How do we know who we are in the Dance?
The dancer, or the world around us in beautiful flight.

The mountains are the corps de ballet.
Silence the music. And all life, the dance!

Look to the past for your feet.
To the present for your body and mind.
And to the future for your reeling heart.
What have you found?

Look again.
And know yourself as a whole man or woman,
an earthquake, or a blade of grass.
In love at the center of the dance!

LEVITATION

*"...I did not even try to explain anything to
myself, so strong was the impression of the
vast, unknown fields opening up before me."*
-G.I. Gurdjieff

How easily the old table moves
to the touch of our family of hands.
Alone, or in pairs
we only gather here to partake in the ritual of food.
Travelers in the history of a day's work.

Only on special evenings at those perfect times
each year when we all meet
do the spoons and bowls get their chance
to dance. And the still and starry night
outside those ancestral rooms sits cross-legged
in the lotus of the heavens in trance.

With age we learn to rise above our needs.
To make do with a good meal and a wish.
To watch carefully how the pendulum swings
in the corner on the old clock. And
the way the candle flickers from its own breath
on an evening without wind.

For a million years we have gathered like this
around tables made of rock and of wood.
In families. Raising our voices in prayer.
Talking to the men and women of night. Until
the sun comes up over the mountains.
And we dream of perfect islands of love,
and are there.

THE EARTH IN A DRAGON'S EYES

"That which is truly Real is given and received in Silence."
-Meher Baba

Only death lights wild candles to the night.
The way that breath
washes away blood. And in that silence
Beauty is forever born!

Where do we go when we want to see God?
To the mirror or to the mind of the Master?
To the photograph or to the face
of the one we love?
The dream we are always chasing
is not found in great movies, in churches,
or in beautiful books.
It is in the earth in the dragon's eyes.
And in the final stillness
of the body stopped at the end of the dance.

There is a voice
beyond the voice of the one we love, that sings.

Listen to the sound breath makes
as it dances with blood!
How the water sleeps
beneath the silk skin of the lake.
Or the quiet voice of the moon
as it screams eloquence, as silence,
to the sounds of peace in the night.

Listen!
To the sound of drumming. To the sound of bells...

THE WHOLE MAN

Like a veil of brown salt had been sent from the Sun,
the ghost of goodness weeps
as perfection disappears from the face of the Earth.
An empty garden
desperate for the birth of food.

Even the stars are chasing their tails.
As they teach their children of the history of night:
How light stops,
and at that moment
becomes stone.

And I am witness to
the prayers of
the silence of
the streets of glass.
How from inside the house of flesh
the windows shatter to the music of dawn.
To the birth of the whole man...
...The coachman dreaming of perfection
and peace as he rides up high on the coachseat.
The carriage as it shakes between
health and being barely alive.
And the horse that weeps
from the whip and a lack of grain.

Where is the wolf that walks
alone in the woods with the lamb?

THE WHOLE MAN

Who walks into town like a festival of mirrors and light
as life in the busy streets stops.
Who, in the heart of this draught,
becomes bread!

Like snow after the morning sun,
the world of ignorance melts. And
the shattered man-body of glass is swept aside.
By the coachman.
Or the woman behind mirrored glass.
As he is slowly moved by what deep inside
he loves!

SYREN

Perhaps
only the one who hammers wood,
gently chisels torso and thigh
into a smoothsilken dream of sex,
can truly see the sunlight in dawn.
And the artist,
like she who sells her body for the seeds of night,
can know, can smell with skin
the perfumed passing of wind.

Not even Narcissus seems to see
anymore the angels from the water
that reflects his face. Playing there
in the quiet pool of river that
begins in his eyes.

Here near the idols of my own sleep
is the sacrilege of the ancient memories
in bone.
And wherever I may find myself
imagining I am
there is a voice coming from out across distance
which like gentle lightning

is showing me the way.

THE SACRED

The seed of spirit is in the flower.
And the flower lives in the garden of all things.

Nowhere has the rock or the wood
become so fertile as in the womb of the earth.
In the hands of plants.
And in the stormy dreams of the gods.

Like the farmer who tills sand along the shoreline of the sea
or poets without ink,
we are born into this world of grace.
With only the seeds of memory and a song
of our ancient race.

Through the warm tears of love
the eyes of fire in the mountains dance.
How quickly the mind becomes water
as we gaze at the moon!
This silver
that lays side by side with gold in the poem of night.

And like the dew, this moon will pass away.

EVERYTHING IS SACRED!